THERE IS AN OLD WILLOW TREE

that presides over an interior garden.

It is a battered tree,

long suffering and much climbed,

held together by strands of wire

but beloved of those who know it.

In a way it symbolizes the city:

life under difficulties, growth against odds,

sap-rise in the midst of concrete,

and the steady reaching for the sun.

Whenever I look at it nowadays,

and feel the cold shadow of the planes,

I think: "This must be saved,

this particular thing,

THIS VERY TREE."

—E. B. White,

Here Is New York, 1949

Dedicated in memory
of everyone we lost on
September 11, 2001.

And dedicated to the people who,
after the towers fell,
picked up the pieces,
planted a forest,
and built a new city—
especially my cousin
Stephen Addeo

A STORY OF 9/11, RESILIENCE, AND REGROWTH

THIS VERY TREE

SEAN RUBIN

HENRY HOLT AND COMPANY

NEW YORK

IN NEW YORK CITY there once stood two towers.
For a time, they were the tallest buildings in the world.
Below the towers was a busy plaza.

That's where I was planted.

Most people who came to my plaza had a job in the city.
I had a job, too.

My leaves *gave people shade.*
My branches *gave birds a place to rest.*

And each year,
I was one of the first trees **to blossom**.

My flowers let everyone know
that *spring was coming*.

Some trees like a quiet park or forest,
but I was a city tree.
   I liked the sound of wind rushing
between the tall buildings.
   I liked the smell of rain
on concrete in the summer.
   I liked being in my plaza,
watching everyone
      coming
         and going.

I was in my plaza the day it happened.

It was an ordinary morning.

Until it wasn't.

I waited there, alone.
Around me it was
dark
and hot
and close.

Did the sun even exist anymore?

It was weeks before they found me.

When I came back into the light,
I knew that everything had changed.
The new noises and smells of
the city scared me.
They reminded me of
what had happened.

Some people put me on a truck and
drove me to a nursery in a faraway park.

I was grateful to be somewhere quiet.

I had changed, too.

All winter, the people at the nursery took care of me.
No one knew if my leaves would come back.

They did.

It was peaceful in the park.
I was surrounded by other trees.
Birds still visited me.
That first spring, a dove made
a nest in my branches.

Years passed. I regrew.

I wondered if my city was regrowing, too.

Sometimes, when a shadow passed overhead,
I thought about what had happened.

But being surrounded by the other trees made
me feel stronger.

Some days, I even felt strong enough
to do my old job again.

That's when I knew I was ready.

It was time to go home.

A machine came to pull me from the ground.
The noise scared me. Leaving scared me even more.

We drove downtown through the city. Now I was worried to go back.
What if something bad happened again?

I already missed the other trees.

Then I saw it.
One shining spire, and many
more towers, surrounding a new plaza.

And in the plaza,
they had planted a forest.
It was filled with *TREES.*

Between the trees, they saved three empty spaces.

Two spaces remained where the towers once stood. They would stay empty forever, because nothing could fill them.

The third space
was for me.

I wasn't comfortable at first.

It had been so long since I'd heard
the wind between the buildings
or smelled wet concrete.

But I was still surrounded
by other trees, and that made me
feel stronger.

I had a new job now, too.

Anyone who felt a shadow overhead
could stand under my leaves and *find peace.*
Anyone who was hurt could see
how my branches had healed and *find hope.*
In my plaza,
filled with so many trees,
I am still
the first

to blossom.

And everyone who sees my flowers
knows that *spring will come*.

AUTHOR'S NOTE

I grew up in New York City. For me, like many people who lived there before 9/11, the Twin Towers were a sort of fixed point in the skyline and in my imagination. I had visited the World Trade Center on a kindergarten class trip, but my strongest images of the towers were from a distance. I can still remember riding in my parents' car and seeing that first view of lower Manhattan across the Brooklyn wetlands, where the Twin Towers seemed to rise from the water of New York Harbor.

I first heard about the Survivor Tree from my agent, Marietta Zacker, and my editor, Christian Trimmer, who asked whether I'd consider writing and illustrating a book about 9/11 and the tree. Like the Survivor Tree, I was initially hesitant to return to this particular place and moment in time. After learning more about the tree, I realized this was an extraordinary creature, so much like a human, with a body and limbs that could be broken and healed, and with a life expectancy of around eighty years that was nearly cut short by tragedy. The Survivor Tree is a living thing that faced death and somehow made it through, not unscathed but alive and continuing to grow. It was healed through its own inner strength and with the care and support of its community. I recognized the Survivor Tree as a friend and neighbor from my hometown. Here was an incredible opportunity to tell the story of 9/11,

and of a trauma survivor, in a way that felt appropriate for children.

The 9/11 attacks happened a few days into my first month of tenth grade. As the years pass, my feelings about that tragedy return more and more to the emotions we felt in the first days and weeks after the towers collapsed, when 9/11 felt like an attack on the New York metropolitan area, and the cleanup was a problem that was ours to solve. The fires were put out by our friends and family, and the rubble was cleared by our neighbors. My cousin Stephen Addeo was a safety inspector on the site.

For a city that prides itself on resilience, 9/11 proved this was no empty boast. New York was battered and broken, and we would take years to heal, knowing many wounds would never disappear. But we were still there. In one episode of the tree's life not included in this story, the Survivor Tree was uprooted in a violent storm in spring 2010, while it was living in the Bronx. It was soon replanted, and eventually made it to the 9/11 Memorial in perfect health. Thinking about the tree's life, Richie Cabo, a horticulturist at the Arthur Ross Nursery, concluded that the Survivor Tree and its surrounding community have a lot in common: "I think of the way the city bounced back and the way the tree keeps bouncing back. It's a New Yorker."

Sean Rubin
Lewis Mountain
Autumn 2020

A BRIEF HISTORY OF THE WORLD TRADE CENTER, 9/11, AND THE SURVIVOR TREE

The World Trade Center stood near the southern tip of Manhattan Island, overlooking the traditional lands of the Lenape people, in a part of New York City called the Financial District. Workers completed the first six buildings of the World Trade Center in 1973, and a seventh building was added in 1985.

The most famous buildings in the World Trade Center were called the Twin Towers. When these skyscrapers were completed, they were the tallest buildings on earth, standing at 1,368 feet and 1,362 feet. (The North Tower was six feet taller than its twin.) The towers were accessed through a plaza, which is an open public area in the middle of a town or city. On a typical weekday, some 50,000 people worked in the various buildings, and another 40,000 visitors passed through on vacation and class trips, or just to take photographs. The plaza

was home to a number of trees, including a Callery pear tree, planted there in the 1970s.

Callery pears are deciduous, which means they shed their leaves each year. The species is native to East Asia, so like many other residents of New York, Callery pears are immigrants to the city. These trees are often planted in urban areas because of their unique shape. With straight trunks and branches that grow high above the street, Callery pears are an ideal shade tree for plazas and sidewalks. They are among the first trees to herald spring in the city, blooming in late March or early April with thick bunches of small, snow-white flowers.

The story in this book is told from the perspective of a real Callery pear tree that would become known as the Survivor Tree. Its life, and the lives of so many throughout the world, changed suddenly on Tuesday, September 11, 2001. On that day, terrorists hijacked four planes in flight. Two planes were flown into the Twin Towers, causing their collapse. Another plane crashed into the Pentagon in Virginia, just outside of Washington, DC, and the fourth plane crashed into a field in Pennsylvania, after passengers resisted their hijackers. This tragedy resulted in the deaths of 2,977 people and left more than 6,000 injured. Many more would become sick from inhaling dust and toxic chemicals released when the buildings collapsed.

The towers' rubble covered the World Trade Center plaza and the surrounding area in 1.8 million tons of wreckage. This area became widely known as Ground Zero, although the people who worked

there called it "the pile." More than 91,000 rescue and recovery workers, including nearly the entire Fire Department of New York, began a cleanup operation that lasted nine months.

In October 2001, workers discovered the Callery pear tree buried underneath the rubble, between buildings four and five of what had been the World Trade Center. The tree was severely damaged. Its roots had snapped and its branches were burned and broken. Although its chance of recovery was slim, the tree was given to the New York City Department of Parks and Recreation in hopes that it could be healed. A month later, the tree was replanted at the Arthur Ross Citywide Nursery in Van Cortlandt Park in the Bronx. For nine years, workers at the park carefully nursed the tree back to health.

By April 2003, the pile had been cleared away and the city began to think about the future. An international competition to create a memorial at Ground Zero was announced, calling for designs that "honored the victims, spoke to the needs of families who had lost loved ones, and provided a space for healing and reflection." In early 2004, a winner was chosen: *Reflecting Absence* by architect Michael Arad and landscape architect Peter Walker. In the footprints of the old towers, two pools were created. Water rushes down the sides of the pools and disappears into voids at the center. Surrounding the pools are bronze slanted walls that list the names of those who died in the 9/11 attacks and in the 1993 World Trade Center bombing.

A new plaza was designed to surround the memorial. While the original plaza had little greenery, the new space would feature 400 swamp oak trees. Looking down on the plaza

are the buildings of the new World Trade Center, including the 1,776-foot One World Trade Center tower, now the tallest building in the Western Hemisphere.

Meanwhile, the Survivor Tree was returning to life. From the scarred stump and broken branches, the tree regrew. Smooth new branches reached for the sun, and small white flowers began to bloom once again each spring. The decision was made to include the tree in the 9/11 Memorial. In December 2010, nine years after it was buried in rubble, the Survivor Tree returned to the World Trade Center and was planted in the new plaza. Today, seedlings of the Survivor Tree are sent all over the world to communities suffering from recent tragedies. These trees, like their parent, continue to stand as symbols of resilience, strength, and hope.

A NOTE ON THE ILLUSTRATIONS

Although the illustrations in this book were created to be as true to life as possible, certain creative license was taken, especially with the timeline of the Survivor Tree after 2009. The construction of the new World Trade Center was also accelerated (an outcome many New Yorkers would have no doubt preferred). In all cases, when I used images that differed from the actual timeline, it was done intentionally to better depict the tree's emotional journey from trauma to recovery. For example, the tree was transferred from the Bronx to the 9/11 Memorial Plaza in December 2010. In the book, I chose to have it arrive in a plaza filled with green trees, as opposed to bare branches, to better capture a feeling of renewal and possibility. (At that time, neither the plaza nor One World Trade Center had been completed.) Finally, the designs of certain buildings and locations throughout this book have been simplified, and distances have been compressed, as to not overwhelm the reader.

A Note on Design

This book was set with Gotham and Adobe Garamond typefaces, chosen because they appear on the cornerstone of the current One World Trade Center. Gotham was designed by Tobias Frere-Jones and Jesse Ragan in 2000; Garamond is based on the designs of the 16th century engraver Claude Garamond.

. . .

Selected Sources

Elliott, Scott. "The 9/11 Survivor Tree Returns Home." *New York Times*, March 26, 2015. nyti.ms/1EXNftD.

Elliott, Scott, dir. *The Trees*. 590films, 2016. Aired September 8, 2016, on *Treasures of New York*, PBS.

Lauinger, John. "Scorched 'Survivor Tree' Rescued from Ground Zero After Attacks to Get New Home at 9/11 Museum." *Daily News* (NY), September 6, 2010. nydailynews.com/new-york/scorched-survivor-tree-rescued-ground-zero-attacks-new-home-9-11-museum -article-1.438376.

National 9/11 Memorial & Museum. "Survival Tree Seedling Program." 911memorial.org/visit/memorial/survivor-tree/survivor-treeseedling-program.

National 9/11 Memorial & Museum. "The Survivor Tree." 911memorial.org/visit/memorial/survivor-tree.

New York City Parks. "Callery Pear." New York City Street Tree Map. tree-map.nycgovparks.org/treemap/species/71298.

. . .

Acknowledgments

Special thanks to Marietta Zacker, Christian Trimmer, Mark Podesta, and Jen Keenan. Thank you to my wife, Dr. Lucy Guarnera, for suggesting that the survivor tree experience its trauma and recovery as a human would and then teaching me what that would look like. Thanks always to E. B. White for a lifetime of inspiration, empathy, and linguistic economy.

Henry Holt and Company, *Publishers since 1866* • Henry Holt® is a registered trademark of Macmillan Publishing Group, LLC • 120 Broadway, New York, NY 10271 • mackids.com • Copyright © 2021 by Sean Rubin • Photographs on pages 46,47 from the Carol M. Highsmith Archive, Library of Congress, Prints and Photographs Division. • All rights reserved • Library of Congress Cataloging-in-Publication Data is available • ISBN 978-1-250-78850-4 • Our books may be purchased in bulk for promotional, educational, or business use. Please contact your local bookseller or the Macmillan Corporate and Premium Sales Department at (800) 221-7945 ext. 5442 or by email at MacmillanSpecialMarkets@macmillan.com. • First edition, 2021 • The illustrations for this book were created using HB graphite pencil and five kinds of erasers on Strathmore 400 bristol board, then scanned and painted on Adobe Photoshop CC. • Printed in China by 1010 Printing International Limited, North Point, Hong Kong • 10 9 8 7 6 5 4 3 2 1